HOW TO MASTER EMAIL MARKETING

YOUR 1-PAGE MARKETING PLAN TO GROW A MASSIVE EMAIL LIST, MAKE MONEY AND BUILD YOUR BRAND WITH EMAIL

BY SMART READS

I0478376

Free Audiobook

As a thank you for being a Smart Reader you can choose 2 FREE audiobooks from audible.com. Simply sign up for free by visiting www.audibletrial.com/Travis to get your books.

Visit:
www.smartreads.co/freebooks
to receive Smart Reads books for FREE

Check us out on Instagram:
www.instagram.com/smart_readers
@smart_readers

ABOUT SMARTREADS

Choose Smart Reads and get smart every time. Smart Reads sorts through all the best content and condenses the most helpful information into easily digestible chunks.

We design our books to be short, easy to read and highly informative. Leaving you with maximum understanding in the least amount of time.

Smart Reads aims to accelerate the spread of quality information so we've taken the copyright off everything we publish and donate our material directly to the public domain. You can read our uncopyright below.

We believe in paying it forward and donate 5% of our net sales to Pencils of Promise to build schools, train teachers and support child education.

To limit our footprint and restore forests around the globe we are planting a tree for every 10 hardcover books we sell.

Thanks for choosing Smart Reads and helping us help the planet.

Sincerely,

Travis & the Smart Reads Team

TABLE OF CONTENTS

INTRODUCTION

Email marketing's reputation has been hanging by a thread for the last few years. Marketers have slowly stopped using it, citing it as a fad that has had its day. Potential subscribers have also stopped subscribing, seeing email marketing as spam or fraud tactics.

Email marketing, then, has seen better days. It's been in better shape.

Well, all the above is what its detractors would prefer you to believe anyway.

The truth is that email marketing is NOT dead. It's still alive and kicking. It's going through its own renaissance right now, as marketers realize customers have not abandoned email at all.

As it turns out Facebook has not killed email marketing.

In this ebook, you'll learn how important email marketing is to your online marketing strategies. it'll show you how to catch the attention of your subscribers with catchy emails that cast you as authority on the subject matter, making them want to sit up and take notice of what you have to say - every single time you say something! When you're an authority on anything, people will listen.

Therefore, if you can present yourself as an authority via email, you will have a much better chance of enjoying success.

Excited? Great. Let's get started!

CHAPTER 1: EVERYTHING YOU NEED TO KNOW ABOUT EMAIL MARKETING

Public opinion is saying something about email marketing. It's saying it doesn't work - plain and simple. But public opinion is also saying something totally opposite to the facts: Email marketing, when done properly, is actually a powerful tool that can boost your sales.

It's still one of the most potent marketing tools on the planet that could turn your business around for the better.

The reason email marketing was such a success for businesses in the first place was because email is so personal. When people receive mail with their name on it, they feel a sense of attachment to it. It's addressed to them, and nobody else.

So why would this change? It hasn't changed! As long as you're still sending an email with permission, the person who receives it will still feel the same sense of attachment.

"Dear Michael, How are you feeling today? We hope you're feeling as good as we are!"

Michael, who is being addressed directly by someone he personally subscribed to, feels a little bit special. You are communicating one-on-one with him. You aren't talking to him and his friends, or him and a thousand other social media users. You're talking to just him. This personal nature of emails can't be replaced - and neither can it go out of fashion.

Indeed, studies have shown customers prefer email more than any other channel of communication when it comes to interacting with businesses. And undoubtedly the number one reason for this is because of how personal email is, as well as the fact that the individual subscribed to the email newsletter in the first place.

There is the rub by the way - you can't send emails out to people who haven't subscribed. That's spam, underhand, and will harm your brand. Don't do it. Only send out emails to people who have subscribed.

Email marketing is also cheap. It is in fact the cheapest way to reach your potential consumers. Its return on investment is estimated to be in the region of - get this – 4000%!

That's staggering, right? To get such an amazing return on your cheap investment, though, you have to be an authority in the subject you're talking about.

Why do so many people subscribe to Tai Lopez and not to any other entrepreneur that just started out? Because they believe Tai to be an authority on the subject. And he is. He's worked his way up to the top and is now the person many people turn to when they need advice. If he sends them an email about this or that, they open it and read because it's from Tai, a guy they know is an expert, and who could possibly help to turn their life around.

So you need to take the time to become an expert in your domain. Someone who provides useful, informative content that can solve problems for people. The more often you do this, the more people will find out about you, and the more popular you'll become. As a result, you will sell more.

Naturally, not just any kind of email will produce spectacular results. You need to keep a lid on your pitches so you're always giving value to your subscribers. The last thing you want to do is swamp them with email after email. This will look spammy, and it will get annoying fast.

People want to hear from you - but they don't want to hear from you all the time. They've agreed to receive emails from you, but what they're agreeing to is an appropriate amount. This goes for both the volume of your emails, as well as the amount of advertising.

It's important to point out that building trust with consumers at this early stage is tough. Why? Because, chances are, they've already been burned in the past. There is no maybe they've been burned in the past - they've been burned. That's a guarantee. As such, you have to work hard to earn their trust.

Now, it's not impossible to earn their trust but you need to make sure you're doing the right things. For example, you need to adopt a personable, friendly and positive voice that speaks to them in a way they understand. You also need to consistently provide value and information that matters to them, and which they care about.

CHAPTER 2: PUTTING TOGETHER AN EMAIL MARKETING STRATEGY

Did you know in order to succeed at email marketing you need to put together an email newsletter every single day of the week for the whole year? And then the year after that too?

That's a lot of email newsletters that have to be conceived, drafted, written up, finalized and sent off! But you can only be successful if you put in the effort and time into creating an email marketing strategy first. This has to be done before you send out your first email.

To create an effective email marketing strategy, you need to first know what email marketing is going to do for you. You need to also set goals that are realistic; work out how much content you are going to need; as well as how much all this is going to cost you.

What Does Email Marketing Mean To You?
For the purposes of this book, email marketing is defined as communication between yourself and your subscribers that your subscribers are permitting. Ergo, they have already agreed to you sending them a weekly email newsletter. Your goal is to boost consumer retention, and thus boost sales.

The permission bit is important. If you don't have an email recipient's permission to drop your newsletter in their inbox, they're going to have a negative view of you. They're not exactly going to be best pleased, and it's going to look like spam. It could be the most valuable email they ever receive, but if they didn't ask for it, chances are, that they won't even open it. The email designed to get you a sale will end up getting deleted without second thought.

The short cut route is to send emails out to all Tom's, Dick's and Harry's who haven't subscribed. But it's not the best route, and it will damage your brand. People will say, "Yeah I've heard of so-and-so. They're experts in spam. I'm sick of getting their emails in my inbox. Who are they even?"

Don't be associated with spam. Be vigilant. Do the right thing and get permission before you send out emails. Your long-term reputation is at stake here.

Before you compose your first email, you need to determine what your goals are. Goals give you direction. They give you a clear vision of where you're heading, and therefore what you need to do (and what you don't) in order to get there.

If you start sending out emails without even knowing what your end goal is, you won't have much success at all. To maximize the effectiveness of your emails, first work out WHY you're doing it in the first place.

Choosing Your Goals

To help choose you goals, take some time to answer the following questions now:

1. How is email marketing going to complement my wider marketing goals? How they will they fit into my broader strategy?

2. Will my numerous marketing tactics be closely related or barely related at all?

3. How am I presently attracting visitors?

4. How do I want my email marketing to attract new visitors and customers?

5. How often do I want to connect with my subscribers?

Have you answered these questions? Okay good. If not, go back and answer them now. It will only take a few minutes even seconds, and they will help you to create a strong email marketing campaign that actually works.

If you've answered them, you can now pick goals that are smart and relevant. They should also be measurable, attainable and they should be goals that can be realistically completed within a reasonable timeframe.

In other words, your goals should be **SMART**:

1. **Be Specific** - Any goal you have must be specific if you are to achieve it. Saying something vague like "Oh, I want to create an email marketing campaign" won't get you anywhere because it's not specific enough. You need to filter out anything you don't need and focus entirely on what you do need. You need a clear idea of what your goal is. Be specific with something like, "I want to send out an email newsletter every Monday morning for the next year about subjects that relate to my business, and which will inform and entertain the reader."

2. **Be Measurable** - If you can't measure your goals, you can't work out how successful or unsuccessful they have been. Therefore, you may end up repeating the same mistakes over and over again. Make sure that your goals are measurable, and track them frequently.

Spot anything that isn't working as soon as possible and improve it or dump it altogether. Find what's working and double down on it.

With email marketing, you won't crack the safe straight away with one or two emails. After five or six emails, you'll still be learning and tweaking your methods and content.

3. **Be Attainable -** Is there something stopping you from attaining this goal? If there is, you need to find out what it is and see if you can work out a way of overcoming it.

4. **Be Realistic -** The worst thing you can do at this point as you create your goals is create a goal that is thoroughly unrealistic, and which totally stresses you down the line as you realize your email marketing campaign has broken you. All goals require hard work. But unrealistic goals are those that are not worth it, and which are driving you to the brink of insanity. Although many entrepreneurs don't like to admit it, there are some things that are unrealistic. Be realistic about this. Set a goal that is within reach.

4. **Be On Time -** No goal was ever completed that wasn't set to a schedule. If you don't plan a schedule, and if you don't find a way of fitting your goal into

your schedule, you really will find it hard to complete it. Do you have the time to launch an email marketing campaign right now? If you don't, is there something in your current schedule that you can either postpone or eliminate altogether so you can make time for your email marketing campaign?

On that same vein, you also need to create a timeline. Ergo, you need to make deadlines.

Deadlines are awesome because they hold you accountable. They give you a concrete timeframe to aim for. Without deadlines, when do you think you will complete your goal? Today? Tomorrow? Next year? You might wake up and decide that you won't work on your goal today because, after all, you don't even know when it's due to be completed. "Sometime in the future," you say.

Without a timeline and without a deadline, your work will never get off the ground.

Take A Look At Your Process Right Now
Take a look at how you're currently generating new eyes to your site or customers into your store. You need to find where your weakest links are. What is stopping you from getting more customers? Why aren't they coming to you?

For example, let's say you run an online store. Let's imagine for a moment that you've made a sale. Once the sale is almost complete, the customer is taken to a confirmation page. They're happy with their purchase, and now they're going to get it confirmed, before they crack on with the rest of their day.

But do you see what's wrong with that scenario?

Just taking the customer to a confirmation page and nothing else is a tad cold. It creates an impersonal shopping experience. It strikes the consumer that you just want their cash and nothing else. It doesn't really make them want to come back in the future.

Not just this, but you're also short changing yourself. You could be doing so much more to keep the customer on the page, or to at least make them want to come back again next time for all their shopping needs.

Not just this, but a confirmation page is so clinical. What if they need a bit more time before making their decision?

This is where email marketing comes in handy. With email marketing, you can track the customer currently buying from you, while also getting info about potential customers so that you can keep your store at the forefront of their minds. So when they do decide that they need to buy something, they think of you.

Not everyone will hand over personal info so easily, of course. But by adding email marketing to your strategies, you're taking that crucial first step towards building a strong relationship with your customers so that they go from being one-time customers to loyal, lifetime ones.

Create The Right List
Once you know where you are right now, as well as where you need to be, you can begin to dedicate time and effort to creating a list of emails and start working on regular content.

If you've already got a website that's been up and running for some time already, you probably have a good amount of info that you can use to create emails your regular customers will want to read. Work out what information you already have, and then you can figure out the information still needed to fill the gaps.

At this point, it's a good idea to create a sign-up widget on your site for your newsletter. You should also include the option to sign-up to your email newsletter as soon as a customer has made a purchase. After all, if they're happy with their purchase, they're feeling good, and as such they're likelier to sign up to your newsletter.

When you gather together data on your consumers, you need to find out certain key information about their demographics. For example, you will need to know their age, their location, their income, their marital status, and even the number of children they have. You will also need to find out what their interests are, their buying history, as well as anything else you can think of that relates to your niche. Essentially, you are building a profile of what your core customer looks like and what they want, need and enjoy.

You'll probably find that you don't have one archetypal customer. For example, it's unlikely that most of your customers will be the same age, the same sex, and have the same interests, live in the same area and have the same amount of kids while also being called David. Instead, it's likely that you will have to divide your core customers into subgroups.

How Are You Going To Gather Your Data?

Okay, so let's imagine that you now know the type of info you need to get from your customers or users. All that's left is to figure out how to go and get it.

Hmm. Tricky! But fear not.

There are two ways you can go about the process:

1. You can try and get all the info you need in one go.

2. You can spread the process out.

There are many ways in which you can gather together key info about your customers:

•On your confirmation page after a customer has just made a purchase
•In one of your emails that you send out to subscribers
• On a questionnaire you send out once every few months
• Or you invite subscribers to update their info once a year

You may also want to give your subscribers a friendly reminder that it'd be great if they could share the newsletter with their friends. The link to your signup page should also be included in all your advertising materials, as well as any business emails you send out.

It's not enough you understand all the data you're going to be collecting. You will also need to have an idea of what you'll be doing with it all once you've collected it. Unless you use it properly and get the most out of it, collecting it in the first place will be totally pointless. Indeed, it will be left to gather dust on your shelf.

Also, it's key that you create proper infrastructure as soon as possible so that key info isn't lost in all the myriad of information you've gathered.

CHAPTER 3: PLANNING FOR CONTENT

A few of the proceeding chapters will explain what you need to be writing. But before you put pen to paper (so to speak), planning your content creation schedule is a good idea.

Decide to create or plan at least two months into the future. Why? Because it takes awhile to create content. Knowing in advance what you'll be writing gives you enough to get it all written down, as well as of course come up with the initial ideas.

Moreover, creating content takes a long time. This is another reason why it's a good idea to plan ahead. And don't forget that you need to work out just how much content will go into each of your newsletters, and well as which products will relate to which newsletter.

Some people enjoy reading long newsletters, as they feel as though it's giving them a lot of value. But the truth is that most customers prefer short, snappy, and concise newsletters that are no longer than a page without formatting, and two-to-three pages when formatted. They like to see lots of white spaces, and they LOVE short paragraphs.

They don't want to be greeted by huge walls of text. It just looks unreadable and off-putting.

If a newsletter is taking up too much of your time, it's probably too long. Shorten it. You don't want your newsletter to take over your entire business. It's meant to boost sales, not consume your life.

Examine The Metrics
Let's imagine you've launched your newsletter and sent a few out. Awesome. At this point, you'll want to know how well it's doing. How many people is it reaching? To do this, you need to examine the metrics.

The first thing you'll want to take a look at is the open rate of the emails. If you're providing the ideal blend of sales and content, this rate should be pretty high.

Next, you will want to take a look at how many people went straight from reading the newsletter to visiting your website. These are called click throughs - an individual is "clicking through" the newsletter and into your website, and perhaps they're clicking through more pages once there.

You will also want to take a look at how many individuals followed what your email was telling them to do, which is what we call source conversions. You can take a look at how many individuals shared the email with others, too. Metrics will be discussed at a later chapter.

CHAPTER 4: WHY IT'S IMPORTANT TO BE AN AUTHORITY

Your content needs to offer the reader lots of value - so much value that they keep reading.

People say that to sustain a reader's interest, you need to be engaging and maybe even entertaining. A novel writer certainly has to be these two things. But you're in sales. As such, you need to add something called value - and lots of it.

When you add value, people treat you as an authority on a subject. And when they start seeing you as an authority, they will trust you.

Sustaining a reader's interest is important because if they don't stick around long enough, they won't get to the part where you're trying to sell them something. And that's the key thing here - with your emails, you're trying to keep individuals on the page long enough for them to reach the part where you try to make a sale.

How can you do this? With a three-pronged attack that consists of:

1. Ethos
2. Pathos

3. Logos

Let's deal with logos first.

Logos is the reasoning for why you draw the conclusions you do in such a way that makes it pretty obvious that the reader should care about what you've got to say about the things you're selling. The goal here is to come up with hypothetical situations which give your subscribers the chance to reach the answer that you always wanted them to reach with the info you gave them.

Any trust you create by virtue of being such an authority is especially key when it comes to logos. Why? Because it gives what you're saying a dimension of credibility.

Pathos deals with tapping into the emotions of your readers. Your aim should be to make them feel a certain way. At first, you might find it tricky to change the way someone feels - but once you have learned more about your customer, it should be easier.

Each piece of content should be written with the aim of making your customer feel a certain way. Don't tell them a pair of sunglasses have this or that feature. Let them know these sunglasses will make them the coolest cat by summer time.

Ethos is all about building your reputation and selling yourself in the niche you're entering. It's all about working on your credibility so people turn to YOU when they need help with a problem related to your niche.

You might have this already, but you might not have. You might have a ton of knowledge on a particular subject, but that's not enough right now to make you an authority figure on it. To become an authority, you need to establish trust with your audience until eventually people see you as their go-to source whenever they need some information.

This will take time - perhaps a lot of time. But through effort and hard work, the rewards will come.

What Does Being An Authority Mean?
Becoming an authority in your niche is hugely important. Once you're an authority, your merry band of loyal followers and subscribers will only keep increasing. It won't decrease (not unless you pull an ill-judged publicity stunt steeped in controversy.) It'll just keep getting bigger.

Of course, be realistic with your expectations. Becoming an authority is difficult and there is no magic pill. What's more, what works for one person, may not work for you. But there are three things you can do to increase your chances:

1. You need to be visible on Google. When someone types in your name, what you WANT them to see has to be among the top results. And it must be very clear that this is you and not someone who shares your name.

2. You need to have a strong presence on social media. Get yourself on Twitter, Facebook, Instagram and LinkedIn; post, comment, share advice and pictures. Grow your brand on these channels. It isn't so difficult.

3. You also need to generate relevant leads. This one is a bit tougher.

When being an authority is mentioned, this isn't the same as being an expert. In the world of online marketing these are two different things and being an expert is not as important as being an authority.

Why? Because an expert is just someone with a lot of knowledge on something. An authority, meanwhile, is the first person people go to when they need that knowledge. It's the person even the experts agree should be sounding out first and foremost.

You could say you're an expert and people might agree. But it's not up to you to say that you're an authority. That's up to other people.

What Are The Advantages Of Being An Authority?
What could be a better benefit than when you speak, people immediately listen? Maybe when you post something, people share it with others straight away. Yeah, that's possibly better.

When you are an authority on something, people pretty much take what you are saying as a given. They believe it to be correct. They don't question it because you're an authority. As you can imagine, this will work wonders for your sales. If you can get into a position whereby you're the authority in your niche, great! Even if others come along who try to topple you, you'll have a band of loyal followers who are willing to defend you.

It's key that you have a good social media presence when you're trying to market your website and establish online presence. You also need to know enough about SEO to drive more traffic and explore different revenue streams (if you don't know much about SEO, either learn all about it or hire someone). Once you become an authority in a particular niche, you don't need to spend so much time chasing down revenue streams, as they tend to just come to you by this point.

At this point you might think there's too emphasis on the idea of being an authority in a particular niche. But just stop for a second and think of any niches you take part in. Then think about the authorities in that niche. A niche could be a political affiliation and the authority could be an online commentator. For example, if you consider yourself to be a member of the alt-right, there might be someone on YouTube and Twitter who is your go-to person for news and information.

This is who you're aiming to become in your niche. The person people turn to when they want info on a certain topic. The person people wake up to in the morning on Twitter, YouTube and whatever other channels you're on.

All You Need Is Trust
The Beatles may have sung that all we need is love, but what you need as you seek to build authority is trust - and lots and lots of it.

No one is going to trust you as an authority figure the first time they see you. They probably won't trust you the second time they see you as an authority figure. But the more they see you, and the more value you offer them, the more they will accept the idea that you are the authority here. You know you're stuff. You're right, and they like that you're right.

Earning the trust of people takes time, just like earning trust and respect in friendship takes time. But guess what? Time is what you have. There is no mad rush here. If you take the time to earn the trust of people who are subscribing to your mailing list, your long-term marketing plan will be a success. Over time, you will experience a fantastic ROI.

Earning trust takes a lot of time. But breaking that trust? That can take just minutes. All it takes is for you to recommend to your followers a cheap product that doesn't work and your reputation is in tatters. And all because you put your name on a flimsy product for a bit of cash. It's not cool at all. Once you do this, you will lose all that trust you built up and you will struggle to get it back (you probably won't ever get it back).

Always value your relationship with your subscribers, and put this and their trust first. Don't go compromising it as you search for short-term profits that will raise questions about your integrity, and also your credibility as an authority.

Studies have shown people trust the content in a newsletter just as much as they trust the person who has written the newsletter. There is a direct correlation. If people feel good about the content, and if they trust it, they also feel good and trust the author.

Before you begin, work on establishing yourself as an authority in your niche, ask yourself if you're presenting yourself in a trustworthy light - or are you presenting yourself in a thin mist, which leaves question marks over your integrity and credibility.

A lot of people struggle with this when they first start out on the long road to establishing trust via email marketing. Think back to any entrepreneurs or social media gurus who have suddenly sprung up from nowhere and presented themselves as an expert in their field. Maybe you were suspicious and decided to do some background checks before validating their authority. Perhaps you Googled their name followed by "scam."

Every person has done it. Anyone who suddenly appears from nowhere, claiming to be experts on a certain topic will be subject to questions and even accusations. If this happens to you, you just need to ride it and do the right things that will help you build a rapport with your audience.

Another really easy way to break the bond of trust you've established with your customers is to mishandle their data. One way to avoid this is to pay close attention to the data you have collected. As you analyze the data, take the time to focus on your loyal customers. Store it safely, and never share it with 3rd party websites. Handling data is important. Whenever there is a data breach, people are put on guard. They get anxious, they worry - and they lose trust. Unfortunately, data breaches happen in our digital age - but they really shouldn't.

But what if no one opens your email? It's difficult to build trust with your audience if you can't even get them to open your emails in the first place!

Studies have shown that one way to encourage people to open your emails is by personalizing them so that they address the person in question. Indeed, people are 40% more likely to open your email if it's addressed to them and not to everyone.

However, it's not enough that you just write "hello, such and such a name."

In 2017, people expect more. Your communication with your customer needs to be even more personal. As such, you need to take the time to add little but significant touches that will improve the chances of them opening the email. Engage them directly. Show you want to talk. Show them that you've got something to share with THEM.

And when you do this, a repeat customer won't just be a repeat customer - they'll also be a loyal follower.

CHAPTER 5: TOP FIVE TACTICS

From now on, your email newsletter will become a key weapon as you set about building your authority. There are two things you need to be aware of right now:

1. How long do you think it will take until you achieve your goal?

2. Around 2,000,000,000 emails are sent out each day. To get any kind of traction going with your own marketing strategies, you need to do something different that gets you noticed.

How To Format A Newsletter
If you thought that sending out a newsletter was as simple as sticking a bit of content into an email first thing in the morning before pressing the send button, you're sadly mistaken. There are a few things you need to do before anything gets sent. Indeed, there are a few things you need to do before you even begin to create content.

Let's go back to what you need to do to make your newsletter more personable. In the last chapter, addressing the recipient with their own name is a good start - but that isn't enough.

A few years back, email marketers thought they'd hit gold when they decided to swap the inclusive "dear all" greeting for the much more exclusive "hey such and such a person."

In many respects, they had struck gold.

The problem is that years have since passed, and being greeted with our names is not enough to convince us to open an email. Why? Because of spam and scams. We are now so accustomed to spammers beginning an email with our name that we tend to think all emails that start with our name are nothing but spam.

This is a bit of a blow to you as an email marketer in 2017, and it can prevent your emails from being opened. In a weird quirk of fate, trying to be personable by using the recipients name in the opening line can damage trust rather than win it.

It's good to establish a tone of familiarity right from the get-go; a tone you would use when addressing people you actually know, but one which is kept in check ever so lightly by a trace of informality.

For example, beginning your email with "inaugural subscriber" strikes the right chord straight away, and you can take it from there. Over time, you can become less informal and more familiar. However, attaining such a level of intimacy must always be earned first.

Naming conventions are hard to nail. It's easier to group people together based on their demographics or purchase history. Purchase history is a really good one. Studies have shown that around 90% of consumers are likelier to respond positively to an email (open it) if it based on their own purchase history.

As you can see, personalization is important. But what's of more importance is that you personalize your emails in the right way. Personalize them in the wrong way and you won't get anywhere. Just one poorly judged email could spell disaster, leaving customers to forever associate you with spam that they don't want anything to do with.

Craft A Winning Subject Line

If there is one thing a subscriber is going to see, it's the subject line. But what's more important? The actual subject line itself and what it's saying, or its length?

As it turns out, it's the length that is more important.

According to studies, people are more likely to respond positively to an email with a short and snappy subject line than they are to one with a long, drawn-out one. It makes a lot of sense when you consider that the average Internet user has the attention span of a goldfish. They make up their mind about something quickly, and they don't have the time to read a long subject lines that can't get to the point fast enough.

A subject line that is no longer than 10 characters are opened 60% of the time. That's a pretty good average. Subject lines that have between 60-70 characters, meanwhile, have no chance of being opened. It's just too long.

It's All About Timing
If you've ever read anything about Facebook ads, you'll have seen people discussing when is the best time to place an ad.

Timing is key when it comes to email marketing, too. If you can send your newsletter out at an optimal time, there is a better chance the recipient will click on your email, open it and take a look.

Studies have been carried out to discover the magic hour - ergo, the best time to send out your newsletters. And they have shown that the best time to send out your newsletters is first thing in the morning. Why? It's because at this stage of the day, people are still free from the stresses that befall them later on. There are fewer things to worry about. They've just gotten up, and their minds are still fresh and receptive to new things. They're not in a bad mood yet!

Another reason why you should press the SEND button early in the day is that there won't be as much ancillary email competing with you. If you send your email out say, at midday, you'll be competing with so many other emails and newsletters. They don't have the time to open and look at everything.

As well as planning what time to mail your newsletter, you also need to think carefully about what day of the week you're going to be sending it out. This is just as important. If you keep sending out your email each week at 11 AM on a Thursday morning, your efforts will always be in vain. It's the wrong time and the wrong day. But how would you know that?

Studies have been carried out to help you optimize your email marketing efforts, and they show that opt-in emails sent out on Friday nights, Saturdays and Sundays all have a better chance of the recipient opening them than emails sent out at any other day of the week.

Newsletters sent out on Saturdays have the best chance of being opened than newsletters sent out on any other day of the week.

Why is this? One reason is that most of your customers probably have the day off work. They've got more time to take it easy and flick through their emails without the stresses of work weighing them down. They're also in a better mood to give your email with the eye-catching subject header a go.

But there is another reason, and again it comes down to what your rivals are doing (or, rather, what they're not doing). Ergo, they aren't sending out their emails on a Saturday. As such, by sending yours out at the weekend, you're avoiding rush hour and slashing the odds of yours being seen and opened.

Give Things Away For Free
People just love free stuff. The entrepreneur Tim Ferriss says that he gives away a LOT of free stuff. The amount of free stuff this guy gives away is quite

incredible. He gives stuff away for free because he knows how much value there is in that.

He's not alone. Many businesses give away a ton of free stuff but they're not losing out. In fact, they're gaining. People love free stuff, and the more free stuff you give away, the more they're going to keep interacting with you. They'll start to associate your brand with feeling good.

Giving stuff away (or at a discount) is especially a good idea if you're struggling to achieve those all-important click-through rates.

Never Forget Mobile Interaction
One of the problems that still befall email marketers in 2017 is content that isn't mobile ready.

You've got a great newsletter, and people are opening it on their desktops. Great. Click-through rates are steadily improving. Fantastic news. But what about the people who are opening your newsletter on their mobiles and can't see the content because it isn't mobile ready?

This is a major error on your part. Content that isn't mobile-ready cheapens your brand - if you can't get your content mobile-ready, it doesn't say much for your professionalism.

Email marketers keep overlooking how important it is that their newsletters are mobile-ready. Never assume that "Oh, they'll take another look at it when they get on their computer." They probably won't.

You need to make sure your newsletter is mobile-friendly because so many people now access their emails with their phones. In fact, studies have shown that people open 70% of emails with their mobile phones!

Remember To Stay On Top Of Your List
A cardinal sin would be to forget all about your list so that it becomes inactive, and therefore totally useless. Let's say you've done very well to build up an email subscriber list. Congrats. But you then need to maintain it. Otherwise, all that hard work is for nothing.

Let's also say you've been sending out emails for a couple of months now and you've noticed a trend. The trend is that half of your subscribers are active, while the other have are inactive.

At this point, you can either give up the ghost with your inactive subscribers or decide that they were never your customers in the first place. Or, you can reach out to them after a few months have elapsed to show them that, during those few months, you've established yourself as an authority in this niche.

See, studies have shown up a rather dismal stat: Around 70% of your subscribers are inactive. That means that way more than half of your subscribers aren't listening to what you're saying. You're losing out on customer, and therefore sales and revenue. So it's important that you reach out to them and try to bring them back in.

How on earth do you reach out to folk that don't want to be reached out to? How do you get them back? They've been inactive for months on end; surely they're not coming back?

Unfortunately, there is no special formula to entire your inactive subscribers back. But there are a few carrots you can dangle in front of them, and one of them is an enticing subject line that guarantees this email - more than any of the previous ones - contains something they're really going to want to read.

Getting your inactive subscribers back will take some time, and you'll need to do some experimenting. It's just a case of figuring out what works and what doesn't. But to be honest, this is what email marketing is all about. Before you launch your first email marketing campaign, all your subscribers are inactive. You have to find a way of hooking them in. And when you've pulled in, say 15% of your inactive subscribers, you still have to think about how to tailor your content so that the remaining 55% get interested.

This is essentially email marketing: tailoring content so your subscribers get something they want to read.

You're not going to get this perfect off the bat. It will take some time before you hit that home run so don't be disheartened.

CHAPTER 6: BUILDING YOUR AUTHORITY

Have You Got The Knowledge?
Whenever you watch a video of someone on Facebook or YouTube talk about a particular subject, you watch it in hopes they're going to drop some knowledge bombs your way. Why? Because you see them as the authority in this particular field.

If you want people to view you in the same way, you have to have knowledge. Ever watched an authority figure respond to a question with a nervous, "Um, I don't know"? Nope! They have the answers because they've done their homework.

To become an authority in your niche, and to make sure you're always sending out emails that offer value to your subscribers, you need to grow your knowledge about your line of work.

If you're line of work is pharmaceuticals, you need to grow your knowledge about pharmaceuticals. You need to know this industry inside out. Always do your homework first. Study. Research. Buy and read books on the subject, check out academic sites on the Internet.

Avoid Wikipedia as much as you can. It's okay for general info, but it's not an authoritative source on any subject. Take notes on what you learn. Weigh things from both angles. Read what experts have said on the subject, and check out studies. Your aim is to develop as much knowledge as possible so you can then start to interpret your knowledge.

And if you ever do a live video on Facebook, you'll have so much knowledge inside you that you can easily answer any question without stumbling and looking fallible. Your aim is to become invincible. People need to trust that you have the answers.

Knowledge gives you confidence, and if you're to become an authority in your niche, confidence is something you will need.

It's important to be realistic here, though. You don't need to know everything about everything. That kind of thing would become exhausting, and it will ultimately be a futile exercise. Learn what is necessary. And then apply your knowledge in the right way.

Choosing A Sub-Niche
In *The 22 Immutable Laws of Marketing,* authors Al Ries and Jack Trout pointed out that it's better to be

the first at something than to be the person who is trying to oust the leader.

This is obvious. If there is already an authority in a niche that people trust, respect and actively seek out, you stand no chance of ousting them. If you come along and decide to dethrone them, you're wasting your time. It doesn't matter how confident you are - you're wasting your time.

So what do you do instead? You either come up with an insanely awesome USP - or you dig further for a relevant sub niche.

Sub niches might not be the first thing you were looking for. But what do they say about gold mines? The further you dig, the greater the riches.

The trouble you might have at first is trying to find the right kind of sub niche. After all, what sub niche is there that needs filling? Who cares about this sub niche?

Google could help. Have a rummage around to see what people are looking for in this niche. Check Google's Keyword Planner to find out what they're searching for. It should give you some clues as to what sub-niches people want to explore, but aren't able to just yet because there is no authority available to give them the information they need.

All niches have some wiggle room for sub-niches, and for a second authority to come along and build their reputation in that sub niche. If you think hard enough about this, and think like there isn't even a box at all, you can find a new, untapped space that people are peering their heads into - but which no one as of yet has come along to establish themselves as an authority.

Picture it like a school. You've got a huge assembly hall that represents the main niche. Inside the assembly hall is a teacher who is teaching hundreds of students all about the main niche.

But you've also got a couple of half-empty classrooms away from the assembly hall. A few students are milling around inside these rooms, wanting information on a sub niche - but there is no teacher to give it to them.

You could be that teacher. Find your classroom, pitch yourself inside it, and start teaching!

There's a story few years back about a small business owner who was looking to try and fill a sub niche. He stumbled upon one about bee keeping. He saw there was a demand for an authority on beekeeping (people were searching for it on Google), but nobody was filling this demand. So, he wrote an eBook on the subject, and positioned himself as the authority figure. And from there, he grew his brand.

Write A Guide
What the guy above did was write a guide about beekeeping and sold it. People bought it first and foremost because it was the only guide of its type on the Internet. And because they bought it, and because it remained the only guide of its type, his reputation grew and he became the authority figure on the subject.

You should think about writing a guide for yourself first. Why? To get to know a subject better, it's helpful to write about it. The more you write about it, the more you'll research it, the more you'll record it - and the more information you'll absorb and remember.

Writing things down helps us remember things, and this can prove invaluable as you seek to become an authority on a particular subject. And the more you write, the more you'll interpret things so that you begin to form your own opinions.

Writing a guide will also improve your mental reflexes whenever you're asked a question on the subject in a live video. You will know your stuff inside out, and you'll be in a stronger position to answer questions with sound answers that make sense.

Get To A Point Where You Can Explain Things Simply

One of the criticisms people have of The Bible is that our world is explained far too simply. How can these monumental events have happened when the science is explained in such simple language? How can we believe a text that covers arguably the greatest ever feat the world has ever seen with such simplicity? Where is the science?

The answer theologians have given is that the scribes who put The Bible together were trying to reach a wide audience - an audience that didn't understand key scientific concepts. An audience that didn't understand physics, matter, gravity, and so on.

They wrote simply and used metaphors and fables so as to make a connection with their audience. And they were pretty successful!

So whether you believe the stories in The Bible or not, what you can't argue with is how beautifully simple they are told. They make an emotional connection with the reader, simplifying the science so that readers of all ages are enchanted. The same readers are so enchanted that they start to believe.

And this is what you need to do with your chosen topic. You need to first understand it yourself, before learning how to communicate it to everyone else in such a breathtakingly simple way so that it is super easy to understand.

You need to become so good at your topic so that whenever a man on the street asks you to explain it to him in 60 seconds and convince him that you know what you're talking about (and so that he knows what you're talking about too!), you are able to do it simply and powerfully. If you can't do this, no one is going to listen to you.

You need to be able to cut through the noise, and break down complicated ideas into simple language that we all understand. Otherwise, you're not going to survive in this world.

This is what marketers do all the time. They've got a few seconds of advertising space they have to somehow fill with their core idea so that a complicated message is communicated in such a way that it is easy to understand and resonates with the viewer.

But it's also important to note here that you shouldn't regurgitate the facts as you see them. That isn't value. What you need to do is take the facts and discuss everything in a compelling, engaging and even entertaining way that people respond to.

Make your delivery unique. Make it funny if possible. Be friendly and personable. Use pictures when necessary.

CHAPTER 7: TAKING YOUR AUTHORITY BUILDING TO THE NEXT LEVEL

Once you've made a connection with your subscribers and sweetened them up, you need to then seal the deal. At this point, their ears are pricked and they're interested in what you have to say. But they don't see you as the authority figure they're always going to turn to when they need information just yet.

This is the moment you double down on your efforts. And once you've positioned yourself as the infallible authority that can't be challenged, it's up to you to maintain your efforts. You can never let your foot off the gas. Once you do, people will quickly forget about you, and a rival will step in.

Look at anyone who has an instantly recognizable brand on the Internet. It took them years to build that brand. And it's going to take them just as many years to maintain it. You simply cannot stop.

Extend Your Reach
By now, you've got a good group of subscribers who see you as their go-to source for information on a particular topic. This is great.

But if you truly want to be the emperor or empress in this field, you will need to leave whatever comfort zone you've got yourself into and branch out even further.

Find new places to put your name so that when your subscribers search for you, they find you in all kinds of different places. Maybe you'll guest blog, or maybe you'll appear on someone's podcast. Or maybe you'll even create your own video. Maybe you'll do a live stream or appear in someone else's live stream. Maybe you'll even find yourself in forums.

Through determination, hard work and a bit of creative thinking, you really can monopolize your niche so much you don't let anybody else in. You've already conquered one land and now you're going to expand. You are not going to sit back, cross your arms and think "Okay, that's that." You're going to totally dominate.

Once you've found another audience, you need to hook them so they, too, subscribe to your newsletter.

Just imagine what guest blogging on a popular blogger's blog could do for your ratings!

People who are new to you will Google you. Make sure you've by now got a strong social media presence, and a strong, credible online footprint that clearly sets you out as an authority.

A quick point about social media: While it can be easy to sit back and tweet aphorisms every now and then from up high in your ivory tower, it's much more advantageous to get out among your people so to speak. Interact with them, answer questions. Take a look at how Gary Vaynerchuck does this. He physically gets out among the people. You can see videos of him giving quick one-to-one tutorials with people while a crowd surrounds him.

Publish A Book
Earlier, you'll recall about the importance of writing a mini guide about the topic you want to master. It would help you to become better at your niche, and to help build yourself as the authority on your chosen field.

You can do the same. You should write the book for yourself, as it will help you to process and memorize all the information you're taking in. But you should also write it with the knowledge you're going to publish it.

Publishing a book (even an eBook) is a fantastic way of quickly boosting your credibility in a niche - especially if people love it and leave positive reviews. Can you imagine what a book with a neat cover and lots of positive reviews will do for your brand? They will supercharge it!

It's not always enough to be some guy or girl who chats about stuff online. Sometimes, people want to see books written by you on the subject - books that have done really well. Books that do well and attract positive reviews display your value. People see the reviews and think "Wow, this person really does offer value."

And then they'll take a closer look at you. So, write a book on the subject, make sure it's awesome, and publish it online.

CHAPTER 8: LET'S IMPROVE YOUR METRICS

Let's say you've tried really hard to position yourself as an authority in your field, but for whatever reason people don't seem to be buying into what you're saying. You take a look at your metrics and they're not great - they're certainly not where you want them to be, or you where you hoped they'd be. So what do you do?

Check Your Open Rate
If you've never been able to get your open rate to where you've wanted it to be, you need to take another look at your subject lines.

Just changing your subject lines - maybe you could talk about the benefits of reading this email as opposed to trying to pique curiosity - can see your open rates success improve by half.

You need to create catchy subject lines that grab peoples' attention. Hook them. Make them fear they'll lose out if they don't click.

Check Your Click-Thru Rate
Okay, so people are opening the emails. But they're not clicking through. Darn it. If this is the problem you've got at the moment, I suggest that you include

some mega-deals on a few of your products - the kind of deals that they really, REALLY don't want to miss out on.

Conversions By Source

Let's imagine that you've managed to position yourself as an authority in your niche. But for whatever reason, your conversions by source are still poor. They're way off base. Hmm.

There are a few things you need to take a look at this point. Check your HTML email. What are you using? If you've got a massive picture, that picture might not be loading on a lot of peoples' phones.

Or maybe you're offering people a load of choices - too many. They can't make their minds up! You could even freshen things up by disappearing for a while, before returning ready to win, with a timely reminder to your subscribers that you're back, better than ever.

CONCLUSION

Ask anyone who has a strong online presence what they think of online marketing and they'll tell you that it works. It's awesome. You HAVE to do it. It's the number one way to position yourself as an authority on a niche and grow your audience.

This book has outlined the steps you need to take to dominate the email marketing scene, position yourself as the king or queen of your niche, and change the game. It's now up to you to take action. The tools are all here for you. Good luck!

THANKS FOR READING

We really hope you enjoyed this book. If you found this material helpful feel free to share it with friends. You can also help others find it by leaving a review where you purchased the book. Your feedback will help us continue to write books you love.

The Smart Reads library is growing by the day! Make sure and check out the other wonderful books in our catalog. We would love to hear which books are your favorite.

Visit:

www.smartreads.co/freebooks

to receive Smart Reads books for FREE

Check us out on Instagram:

www.instagram.com/smart_readers

@smart_readers

Don't forget your 2 FREE audiobooks.
Use this link www.audibletrial.com/Travis to claim
your 2 FREE Books.

SMART READS ORIGINS

Smart Reads was born out of the desire to find the best information fast without having to wade through the sheer volume of fluff available online. Smart Reads combs through massive amounts of knowledge compiles the best into quick to read books on a variety of subjects.

We consider ourselves Smart Readers, not dummies. We know reading is smart. We're self taught. We like to learn a TON about a WIDE variety of topics. We have developed a love for books and we find intelligence attractive.

We found that each new topic we tried to learn about started with the challenge of finding the pieces of the puzzle that mattered most. It becomes a treasure hunt rather than an education.

Smart Reads wants to find the best of the best information for you. To condense it into a package that you can consume in an hour or less. So you can read more books about more topics in less time.

OUR MISSION

Smart Reads aims to accelerate the availability of useful information and will publish a high quality book on every major topic on amazon.

Smart Reads hopes to remove barriers to sharing by taking the copyright off everything we publish and donating it to the public domain. We hope other publishers and authors will follow our example.

Our goal is to donate $1,000,000 or more by 2020 to build over 2,000 schools by giving 5% of our net profit to Pencils of Promise.

We want to restore forests around the globe by planting a tree for every 10 physical books we sell and hope to plant over 100,000 trees by 2020.

Doesn't it feel good knowing that by educating yourself you are helping the world be a better place? We think so too...

Thanks for helping us help the world. You Smart Reader you...

Travis and the Smart Reads Team

WHY I STARTED SMART READS

Every time I wanted to learn about something new I'd have to buy 20 books on the topic and spend way too long sorting through them and reading them all until I arrived at the big picture. Until I had enough perspectives to know who was just guessing, who was uninformed and who had stumbled upon something remarkable.

I wished someone else could just go in and figure that out for me and tell me what matters. That's how smart reads was born. I want smart reads to be a company that does all that research up front. Sorts through all the content that is available on each topic and pulls out the most up to date complete understanding, then have people smarter than me package the best wisdom in an easy to understand way in the least amount of words possible.

For example, I got a new puppy so I wanted to learn about dog training. I bought 14 different books about dog training and by the time I got through the first 5 and finally started getting the big picture on the best way to train my puppy she had grown up into a dog.

Yeah she's well behaved. She doesn't poop in the house. I can get her to sit and come when I call. But what if someone else went in and read all those books for me, found the underlying themes and picked out the best information that would give me the big picture and get me right to the point. And I'd only have to read one book instead of 15.

That would be amazing. I would save time. And maybe my dog would be rolling over, cleaning up after my kids and doing the dishes by now. That my friend, is the reason I started smart reads. Because I wanted a company I can trust to deliver me the best information in an easy to understand way that I can digest in under an hour. Because dog training is one of many subjects I want to master.

The quicker I can learn a wide variety of topics the sooner that information can begin playing a role in shaping my future. And none of us knows how long that future will be. So why not do everything we can to make the best of it and consume a ton of knowledge. And I figured all the better if I can also make a positive difference in the world.

That's why we're also building schools, planting trees and challenging ideas about copyright's place in today's world. Because as a company we have to be doing everything we can to support the ecosystem that gives us all these beautiful places to read our books. Thanks for reading.

Travis

Customers Who Bought This
Customers Who Bought This Book
Also Bought

Understanding Affiliate Marketing: An Internet Marketing Guide for How To Make Money Online Using Products, Websites and Services

Success Principles: Techniques for Positive Thinking, Self Love and Developing a Powerful

Passive Income: Do What You Want When You Want and Make Money While You Sleep

Blockchain Revolution: Understanding the Internet of Money

The Everything Store Sales Guide: How to Make Money with Amazon FBA

Overcoming Procrastination: Proven Strategies on How To Improve Focus, Get Things Done and Achieve Your Goals

Mastering Your Time: Learn How Successful People Enhance Productivity, Beat Procrastination and Do More in Less Time

A Detailed Guide in Building A Successful Photography Business Online: Learn How to Market, Sell, Promote and Make Money as a Photographer